Original title:

Connecting Souls

Author: Kätriin Kaldaru

ISBN HARDBACK: 978-9916-89-103-2

ISBN PAPERBACK: 978-9916-89-104-9

ISBN EBOOK: 978-9916-89-105-6

Bonds Born of Silence

In quiet corners, we reside,
Unspoken words, our thoughts collide.
Soft glances shared, a gentle sway,
In silence, love finds its own way.

The world around fades from our sight,
A shared existence, pure delight.
No need for chatter, no grand displays,
In stillness, our spirits find ways.

Through whispered dreams beneath the stars,
In tranquil moments, healing scars.
Embraced in silence, two hearts align,
Creating bonds, uniquely divine.

Time drifts softly, like falling leaves,
In silence, every heartache cleaves.
The power of touch, a guiding force,
Together we forge our true course.

With every breath, our souls entwined,
In muted realms, our love defined.
A tapestry rich, woven tight,
Bonds born of silence, pure and right.

Weaving Heartstrings

Threads of laughter, spun with care,
In every moment, love lays bare.
Patterns woven, bright and bold,
A story of warmth in colors told.

Each heartbeat hums a sweet refrain,
From joy to sorrow, love remains.
With gentle hands, we pull and weave,
In the fabric of trust, we believe.

A tapestry crafted through time's art,
Every stitch binds, never apart.
In the loom of dreams, we find our place,
Heartstrings connect in a soft embrace.

With whispered secrets, we show our truth,
In the tale of us, capturing youth.
Through trials faced, the threads grow strong,
Weaving heartstrings, where we belong.

Together we dance in the light's embrace,
In every moment, a sacred space.
United forever, as storm clouds fade,
In every heartbeat, our love displayed.

Comfort in Presence

In gentle stillness, we sit and breathe,
A moment shared, no need to leave.
Your eyes, a haven, calm and clear,
In your presence, I feel no fear.

With soft whispers, the world drifts away,
In the warmth of now, we choose to stay.
No grand gestures, just quiet sighs,
Comfort found in shared replies.

Through life's chaos, hand in hand,
Together we build, together we stand.
A knowing smile, a supportive nod,
In mutual silence, our paths have trod.

Days may rush, the hours flee,
Yet in your light, I find my spree.
In simple joys, my heart takes flight,
Comfort in presence, ever bright.

As shadows lengthen and evening falls,
In gentle moments, my spirit calls.
Grateful for you, forever embraced,
In the comfort of love, fear is effaced.

Serene Junctions

Where rivers meet, the waters blend,
In tranquil moments, hearts transcend.
Crossroads of fate, where paths combine,
In serene junctions, love does shine.

Underneath canopies wide and grand,
Time slows down, as we make our stand.
With silent smiles and hands entwined,
Our spirits dance, beautifully aligned.

The world fades out, as we explore,
In the hush of now, we seek for more.
Each whispered breeze, a soft embrace,
In this haven, we've found our place.

In gentle currents, we ride the flow,
Together we journey, letting go.
At every crossroad, choices made,
In serene junctions, fears will fade.

So let us linger, a moment or two,
In the heart of stillness, just me and you.
Together we trace these sacred lines,
In serene junctions, our love defines.

Shadows that Embrace

In twilight's hush, shadows blend,
They weave their tales without end.
A dance of whispers, close yet far,
Embracing light, beneath a star.

Night's soft arms, they cradle dreams,
In silent places, nothing is as it seems.
They cradle hopes with gentle grace,
In shadows deep, we find our place.

The world below, a muted sound,
In darkness, love and hope abound.
Together we stand, hand in hand,
Within the shadows, we take a stand.

Time flows slow, moments linger,
Kindred souls, touch with a finger.
In the quiet, we find our song,
Where shadows dwell, we all belong.

Through the night, we roam so free,
In shadows shared, just you and me.
Beneath the moon, our spirits soar,
In these shadows, we ask for more.

Luminous Connections

In daylight's glow, hearts intertwine,
With every glance, a secret sign.
Laughter dances on beams of light,
In golden moments, pure delight.

Connected souls, in unison play,
Brightening paths along the way.
They spark like stars in a velvet sky,
With every shoulder, we learn to fly.

Through woven tales, our spirits grow,
In luminous threads, warmth does flow.
Every heartbeat echoes the tune,
A melody sung under the moon.

Fleeting seconds feel like a year,
In glowing bonds, we hold so dear.
With whispered dreams and hopes embraced,
Together we shine, our fears replaced.

In sacred spaces, love ignites,
With fervent flames and endless nights.
We rise as one, a radiant sigh,
In luminous connections, we touch the sky.

Threads of Destiny

Within the loom of fate we find,
Threads that twist, yet are aligned.
Weaving stories, rich and bright,
In each pattern, our souls unite.

Every encounter, a stitch in time,
Dancing along with reason and rhyme.
In tapestry woven, dreams reside,
Threads of destiny, side by side.

Paths unknown may lead us far,
Every thread, a shining star.
Faint echoes of choices made,
In the weave of life, none shall fade.

With steady hands and hopeful hearts,
We navigate where journey starts.
In every twist, a chance to grow,
Threads of destiny start to flow.

Together we forge our fate anew,
With colors bright and shades of blue.
In fragile strands, resilience lives,
Through threads of destiny, the heart gives.

As One in Silence

In the quiet, our souls collide,
In gentle whispers, there's no need to hide.
With every heartbeat, we understand,
As one in silence, we take a stand.

Moments linger beneath the stars,
No barrier stands between our hearts.
In stillness vast, we seem to fly,
As one in silence, just you and I.

Time slips by, a fleeting glance,
In sacred quiet, we find our chance.
Each breath a promise, shared and true,
In silence deep, I'll cherish you.

Words unspoken, yet so profound,
In the calm, our love is found.
Beyond the noise of life's embrace,
As one in silence, we find our place.

Through every trial, hand in hand,
In the hush, together we'll stand.
With silent strength, our spirits rise,
As one in silence, beneath the skies.

Whispers Across the Miles

In the hush of night, we speak,
Soft whispers carried, hearts unique.
Across the miles, a tender thread,
Binding our dreams, where love is fed.

Stars above twinkle in delight,
Guiding our thoughts through endless night.
You in my heart, wherever you roam,
In every whisper, I find my home.

The moonlight glows on your cherished face,
A silent promise, a warm embrace.
Though distance stretches, we'll never part,
For every whisper lives in our heart.

In every letter, a dream unfolds,
Tales of longing and love retold.
Through time and space, our spirits fly,
Whispers of love that never die.

So hold me close in your dreams tonight,
Together we'll chase the morning light.
No barriers strong enough to confine,
Two souls in sync, eternally entwined.

The Heart's Cartography

A map is drawn in love's embrace,
Each heartbeat marks a sacred place.
With every pulse, the journey starts,
Charting the realms of eager hearts.

Through valleys deep and mountains high,
We traverse paths where memories lie.
With ink of passion, the lines we trace,
Mapping our souls in a tender space.

Every landmark holds a secret theme,
Echoes of laughter, a shared dream.
Together we wander, hand in hand,
Navigating this vast, wondrous land.

Time is but a gentle guide,
As we explore the tides inside.
In every corner, love's whispers cling,
Navigating through the spaces they bring.

So let the compass spin and sway,
With you beside me, come what may.
Our hearts the map, forever true,
In this cartography, it's me and you.

Infinitely Entwined

In a world where shadows play,
We found a love that guides our way.
Two souls twined, like vines in bloom,
Spreading light, dispelling gloom.

With every glance, our hearts collide,
Dancing together, side by side.
Infinite threads of fate align,
Woven tightly, forever entwined.

Through the seasons, we grow and bend,
In this journey, there's no end.
Like constellations in the sky,
Together, we reach and never say goodbye.

In whispered dreams and starlit nights,
Our love ignites, like city lights.
Each moment shared, a sacred sign,
Two destinies meet, infinitely entwined.

So take my hand, let's brave the storm,
In your embrace, I feel so warm.
Boundless love, a sacred design,
In this tapestry, eternally entwined.

Radiant Intersections

In moments fleeting, we collide,
Where pathways cross, our hearts confide.
A spark ignites at every turn,
In the dance of fate, we brightly burn.

Every glance, a silent vow,
In this sweet chaos, we'll figure how.
With laughter shared, our spirits blend,
In radiant intersections, love transcends.

Through crowded streets, our souls align,
In the tapestry of time, you are mine.
Each heartbeat echoes, a vibrant song,
In a world where we both belong.

As colors merge in a sunset sky,
Our dreams take flight, soaring high.
In intertwined journeys, we find the light,
Radiant intersections, love's pure delight.

So let's embrace the journey ahead,
With open hearts and dreams widespread.
In every twist, our love shall shine,
Forever bound in this grand design.

Chasing Light Together

In the dawn's early hue, we run,
Hand in hand, lost in the fun.
Golden rays guide our way,
Promising hope for a new day.

Through fields of dreams we roam,
Finding in each other a home.
The sun kisses our skin,
In this eternal chase, we begin.

With laughter as our song,
Every moment where we belong.
We dance like shadows pure,
In the warmth of love's allure.

As day fades into night,
Stars twinkle, soft and bright.
Together, we find our sight,
In tales of chasing light.

Close your eyes, breathe in deep,
In this bond, secrets we keep.
With each heartbeat shared anew,
In this chase, it's me and you.

Reflections of the Mind

In quiet moments, thoughts arise,
Like whispered secrets in the skies.
Mirrored visions of what's near,
Conscious echoes we hold dear.

Each memory a brushstroke fine,
Painting stories through space and time.
Fragments of laughter, joy, and pain,
In the gallery where we remain.

Wander through the maze of dreams,
Where nothing's ever as it seems.
Reflections twist, then come around,
In the silence, truths are found.

Moments freeze like drops of rain,
Caught in stillness, joy, and strain.
Each flicker holds a reminder,
In wisdom's glow, we grow kinder.

With every thought, a journey starts,
Mapping the terrain of our hearts.
In the landscape where we reside,
Reflections of the mind, our guide.

Tethered by Fate

In a world vast and unknown,
Two souls meet, seeds are sown.
Ties invisible yet strong,
A melody, an ancient song.

Paths entwined by unseen hands,
Together we navigate distant lands.
With fate's thread woven tight,
We find comfort in shared light.

Through storms and trials that may come,
Our hearts beat in a steadfast drum.
In the tapestry of time we stitch,
Destiny's design, our perfect niche.

Every challenge, hand in hand,
Together we rise, together we stand.
Love's embrace, our timeless thread,
A bond that keeps us warm instead.

As the stars align in the night,
We walk forward, hearts in flight.
Tethered by fate, we advance,
In this cosmic dance, we prance.

Symphonic Understanding

In silent notes, our hearts compose,
A symphony where love just flows.
Every glance, a subtle tune,
Painting colors, bright as noon.

Harmonies in the air we breathe,
A rhythm found, in hearts we weave.
Connect the sounds, so sweet, so clear,
In perfect time, you draw me near.

With every beat, our spirits rise,
Echoes whisper beneath the skies.
Together we create a song,
In this dance, we both belong.

Melodies blend, our souls unite,
Creating magic in the night.
Understanding speaks without a word,
In every note, our love is heard.

As the final chord rings out,
We smile, knowing what it's about.
In this symphony, vast and grand,
Symphonic understanding, hand in hand.

Kindred Spirits in Flight

In the dawn's embrace we rise,
With wings that brush the skies.
Together we soar, hearts entwined,
Two souls in harmony aligned.

The winds of fate guide our way,
In laughter and dreams we play.
Each moment shared, a gentle spark,
Illuminating paths in the dark.

Through valleys deep and mountains high,
We journey on, you and I.
Bound by hopes, our spirits gleam,
In every wish, we dare to dream.

With every beat, our hearts conspire,
To reach beyond, to climb higher.
Together we chase the fleeting light,
Kindred spirits, taking flight.

In the twilight's soft refrain,
We find solace in the rain.
Two lives as one, in a dance profound,
In the tapestry of love, we're found.

Under Starlit Skies

Under starlit skies, we lay,
Whispers of night, a soft ballet.
The cosmos wraps us in its glow,
In silence, our hearts start to flow.

Each star a memory, bright and clear,
A universe shared, you are near.
With every breath, the night unfolds,
Magic woven in tales untold.

Moments stolen, a gentle tease,
Time stands still, a breath of ease.
Bathed in light from celestial streams,
We drift softly into our dreams.

Your hand in mine, a silver thread,
We wander through dreams, where love is spread.
The moon's reflection upon your face,
A timeless bond, our sacred space.

Under this sky, where wishes ignite,
We dance as one, lost in the night.
The universe sings of our ties,
Forever united under starlit skies.

Bridges Unseen

Across the rivers, we build our dreams,
With bricks of hope and golden seams.
Bridges unseen, crafted with care,
Uniting souls from everywhere.

Hand in hand, we face the storm,
In every challenge, love keeps us warm.
The gaps we close, as we explore,
Painting the worlds we both adore.

From peaks to valleys, we take our stand,
Together we roam this vibrant land.
With every step, a promise we weave,
In the tapestry of what we believe.

Invisible paths lie before our eyes,
In trust and faith, our spirit flies.
Through every trial, we find our song,
In the symphony of right and wrong.

Bridges unseen, yet felt so deep,
In the love we share, it's ours to keep.
Each connection made, a thread divine,
In this vast world, your heart is mine.

Together in the Stillness

In the quiet hour before dawn's light,
We find each other, hearts shining bright.
Stillness wraps us in its warm embrace,
In whispered dreams, we find our place.

The world outside fades to a hum,
In this cocoon, our souls are spun.
Each breath a melody, soft and slow,
Together, in love, we gently glow.

Time pauses here, with you by my side,
In the hush of the moment, we confide.
Every heartbeat tells a tale so sweet,
In the silence, our spirits meet.

The universe listens, as we lay low,
Absorbing the peace, allowing love to grow.
A pact unspoken, strong and true,
In every silence, it's me and you.

Together in stillness, we dance with grace,
Finding solace in this sacred space.
As dawn breaks through, we take flight,
In our hearts, we hold the night.

The Fabric of Our Beings

In quiet threads we weave our dreams,
Colors bright, with soft moonbeams.
Each moment stitched, a tale unfolds,
A tapestry rich, in love it holds.

Together we dance on this canvas wide,
With every twist, our hearts reside.
Searching for patterns that time may show,
In the loom of life, our spirits grow.

Through storms and sunlight, our fibers bend,
Yet bound by strength that will not end.
Embroidered whispers, secrets shared,
In the fabric of us, we are ensnared.

With joy in the stitching, a needle's grace,
We find our place in time and space.
Every ripple tells stories anew,
Woven together, forever true.

Notes from a Shared Life

We write our stories, page by page,
In the margins, wisdom of age.
Notes of laughter, tears, and cheer,
In the symphony of life, we steer.

With ink of hope, we draft the lines,
In every pause, our heart entwines.
A melody shared in silence speaks,
In the spaces, love uniquely peaks.

Together we sing, a heartfelt tune,
Under the watchful, whispering moon.
In every chorus, our voices rise,
Painting our journey across the skies.

With each note struck, memories flow,
Binding us tight in the ebb and glow.
As seasons change, we pen our songs,
In the symphony of us, where we belong.

Harmony in the Distance

Across the valley, echoes softly play,
Whispers of love, drifting away.
In the twilight glow, a melody calls,
Across the miles, our spirits enthrall.

Each note a bridge, connecting the space,
In the stillness, we find our grace.
Though shadows linger, hope brightly sings,
In the distance, our freedom springs.

The stars compose their timeless song,
In the silence, we both belong.
A symphony woven with threads of night,
Our hearts in concert, feeling the light.

Through restless dreams, the harmony flows,
In the distance, where love still grows.
Together in spirit, never apart,
We remain in tune, heart to heart.

Harmonies of the Heart

In the quiet hush, where dreams reside,
Our hearts compose, no words to hide.
With gentle rhythms, we sway and turn,
In the dance of love, our spirits burn.

Each beat a whisper, a tale untold,
In the warmth of embrace, together we bold.
With every sigh, an echo so pure,
A melody blossoms, forever sure.

Through valleys low and peaks so high,
Our harmonies blend, under the sky.
In the music of life, our souls unite,
In the symphony of day and night.

With grace we rise, as the sun bestows,
In the tapestry of time, our love grows.
A chorus sweet, in darkness and light,
Harmonies of the heart, our eternal flight.

Circles of Trust

In the quiet of whispers, we share,
Bound by promises, tender and rare.
Hearts open wide, secrets are spun,
In circles of trust, we become one.

Echoes of laughter, moments we save,
Through shadows and light, together we brave.
With every storm, we find our way,
In circles of trust, we choose to stay.

Hand in hand, we journey on,
Through highs and lows, we are drawn.
Each step we take, our bond grows strong,
In circles of trust, we belong.

In the depths of night, fears allayed,
With voices soft, our doubts fade.
Every word woven like a song,
In circles of trust, where we belong.

Together we rise, hand in hand,
Roots entwined, we make our stand.
In the light of dawn, we greet the day,
In circles of trust, we find our way.

Hidden Harmonies

In shadows where whispers softly blend,
Unseen connections begin to mend.
Notes of silence, melodies stay,
Hidden harmonies guide our way.

The rustle of leaves, a soft breeze,
Nature's whisper brings us to our knees.
Every heartbeat, a soothing sway,
Hidden harmonies lead astray.

Stars above in a velvet night,
Glistening dreams spark pure delight.
Their gentle glow promises play,
Hidden harmonies light the way.

Through tangled paths, we wander free,
In the silence, we learn to see.
Life's rich tapestry, bright and gray,
Hidden harmonies find their way.

In the dance of life, let it unfold,
Secrets of the universe whisper bold.
In every moment, come what may,
Hidden harmonies hold sway.

In the Space Between

Between the notes, a silence grows,
In its embrace, the mystery flows.
Each heartbeat echoes, soft and keen,
In the space between, we glean.

Where words are few, connections start,
In tender glances, we share our heart.
A universe rests, calm and serene,
In the space between, we dream.

Moments linger, suspended in air,
Caught in a breath, we pause to care.
Time stands still, we find our sheen,
In the space between, we are seen.

Awareness blooms, a sacred place,
With every sigh, we find our grace.
Uncharted realms, rich and pristine,
In the space between, we convene.

Hands entwined, souls gently sway,
In this haven, we choose to stay.
With every pulse, a love routine,
In the space between, we glean.

Threads of the Infinite

Each thread we weave, a story spun,
In patterns vast, our lives are won.
Colors entwined, bright and dim,
Threads of the infinite, not just whim.

Through valleys low and mountains high,
We stitch together, you and I.
Embracing fate, every whim,
Threads of the infinite, not so slim.

In every choice, a path unfolds,
A tapestry rich with joys untold.
Each twist and turn, a secret hymn,
Threads of the infinite, we begin.

Connections deep, like rivers flow,
With every heartbeat, love will grow.
In the fabric of life, we swim,
Threads of the infinite, let us brim.

So here we stand, hearts intertwined,
With every dream, our hopes aligned.
In the vast expanse, we don't skim,
Threads of the infinite, we swim.

Timeless Affinity

In twilight's glow, we find our way,
Threads of fate that softly sway.
In whispers faint, our hearts align,
Two souls entwined, in love they shine.

Like rivers flow, through mountains high,
Our bond endures, it cannot die.
With every laugh, with every tear,
Timeless joy, forever near.

Through seasons' change, our spirits soar,
In silence shared, we need no more.
In moonlit nights, we share a dream,
Together lost, a perfect theme.

Upon the stars, our hopes are kissed,
In every moment, you exist.
No distance can our hearts defy,
For love transcends, it cannot lie.

Reaching Across the Divide

Between the hills, a call unfolds,
Two hearts apart, both brave and bold.
With open hands, we stretch our arms,
To bridge the space, embracing charms.

In shadows cast, we search for light,
Two souls awaken in the night.
A gentle breeze, a whispered prayer,
In every hope, our dreams laid bare.

Though miles between may often form,
Our spirits dance, they rise, they warm.
With every step, a path we pave,
In unity, we're strong and brave.

Across the seas, a bond takes flight,
Two kindred souls, igniting light.
No hurdles high can hold us down,
For love will wear the victor's crown.

Soulful Encounters

In crowded rooms, our eyes collide,
A fleeting glance, where dreams reside.
With every heartbeat, stories weave,
Two souls ignite, and hearts believe.

Through laughter shared, a spark unfolds,
In silent moments, truth retold.
A touch, a sigh, the world dissolves,
In soulful depths, our mystery evolves.

With every word, significance,
A dance of fate, a sweet romance.
Beneath the stars, our spirits merge,
In every breath, our souls converge.

The universe conspires to bind,
Two hearts awakened, intertwined.
With every glance, a cosmic dance,
In every chance, a timeless trance.

Interwoven Stories

Within the pages, our lives unfold,
Tales of adventure, both brave and bold.
In every chapter, a lesson learned,
Through joy and sorrow, our hearts yearned.

In whispered secrets, bonds are forged,
With every moment, our souls enlarged.
The tapestry rich, in colors bright,
Interwoven dreams, taking flight.

Through ups and downs, our laughter shared,
In every struggle, our love declared.
As seasons change, our stories blend,
In heartfelt words, our lives extend.

With love as ink, we write anew,
Together crafting a vibrant hue.
With every twist, the plot reveals,
The bond of life, in love, it seals.

Threads of Kindred Spirits

In the quiet night we weave,
Thoughts that spark like fireflies,
Connections that we can't perceive,
Binding us, beyond our sighs.

Voices soft, they call my name,
A comfort in the shadows cast,
Through the warmth, we share the flame,
In memories that bind the past.

With every moment shared, we grow,
Roots entwined in earth and sky,
In the dance of life, we flow,
Synchronized as days ripple by.

Kindred souls, forever near,
In laughter and in tender tears,
We gather strength, dispel the fear,
Resilient through the passing years.

Threads that shimmer in the light,
A tapestry of hopes and dreams,
Together we can fight the night,
Through love, we find our quiet gleams.

Tapestry of Hearts

Colors bright and shadows deep,
Woven tales of joy and pain,
In this fabric, secrets keep,
With every loss, a cherished gain.

Fingers trace the patterns fine,
Stories folded in the thread,
In the heart's deep, sacred shrine,
Echoes of the love we've said.

Stitch by stitch, we build our bond,
With each heartbeat, stronger still,
In the tapestry, we respond,
With threads of hope and endless will.

Through the years, the fabric flows,
Moments captured, never lost,
In every seam, this love still grows,
A masterpiece, no matter the cost.

Together we create a song,
In harmonies of dusk and dawn,
With every stitch, we do belong,
A tapestry of hearts, reborn.

Echoes in Harmony

In the stillness, whispers play,
Voices blend like softest rain,
Through the silence, words convey,
Melodies that soothe the pain.

Every note a bridge, a call,
Unified in joyful sound,
In this symphony, we fall,
Where the echoes dance around.

Together, we'll sing our dreams,
With the stars, we weave the night,
In the glow, our passion beams,
Through the darkness, we find light.

Resonating through the day,
Harmony that never fades,
In this chorus, come what may,
We find strength that serenades.

Echoes linger in the breeze,
Carrying our tales afar,
In every heart, a piece of ease,
In harmony, we shine like stars.

Bridges Across Time

In the distance, shadows play,
Footsteps echo in the dusk,
Bridges built, come what may,
Through the layers, strong, robust.

Every moment, carved in stone,
Time, a river flowing swift,
In our hearts, we're never alone,
Bridges formed as we uplift.

Memories flicker, then they rise,
Like lanterns in the endless night,
Across time, love never dies,
Guiding souls with constant light.

Through the ages, hand in hand,
We traverse the span of years,
With a wisdom, gently planned,
Bridges built from hopes and fears.

In our laughter, echoes blend,
Though the years may twist and tie,
In this journey, we transcend,
Bridges strong, that never die.

Harmony of Hearts

In twilight's glow, we find our way,
Two souls adrift, in soft ballet.
Through gentle whispers, love's embrace,
A dance of dreams, in time and space.

With every heartbeat, a silent tune,
Concord among the stars and moon.
Bound by the thread of shared delight,
Together we shine, in love's pure light.

Through storms we've sailed, through trials faced,
In every moment, our bond is laced.
Hand in hand, we brave the night,
In harmony, our hearts take flight.

Each glance a promise, each laugh a chord,
In the symphony of love, we're restored.
With every breath, a melody sweet,
A tapestry woven, where dreams repeat.

In laughter, joy, through pain we grow,
With every challenge, our love will show.
Together we flourish, together we stand,
In the harmony of hearts, hand in hand.

Threads of Essence

In woven strands, our lives entwine,
Threads of essence, both yours and mine.
Bound by stories, both old and new,
In the fabric of time, our colors brew.

Each moment stitched with care and hope,
Through trials faced, in love we cope.
Silken whispers in the night air,
A tapestry rich, beyond compare.

In laughter's echo, the threads grow bright,
In shared silence, we find our light.
Every heartbeat, a gentle seam,
We weave together, in each dream.

Unraveled threads tell tales of yore,
From distant shores to the ocean's roar.
In every knot, a memory lies,
A reflection of love in our eyes.

With every change, our patterns flow,
In the dance of life, we twirl and glow.
Each thread a promise, strong and true,
In this fabric of life, I cherish you.

Whispering Spirits

In forest deep, where shadows play,
Whispering spirits guide our way.
Through ancient trees, their voices soar,
Echoing secrets from days of yore.

With rustling leaves, they softly speak,
In every breeze, their presence peaks.
A gentle touch upon my face,
In nature's heart, I find my place.

Moonlit paths, where magic glows,
In every footstep, the spirit flows.
They dance on air, they twirl on ground,
In every silence, their love is found.

Through swirling mist and starlit skies,
Whispering spirits, they never die.
In twilight's grace, their tales unfold,
In every heartbeat, their whispers bold.

As night descends, I feel them near,
Guardians of dreams, they calm my fear.
With every breath, they intertwine,
Whispering spirits, forever divine.

Unseen Threads

In shadows cast, where light hides low,
Unseen threads weave stories slow.
Each glance a promise, each touch a tie,
In the depths of silence, we learn to fly.

Bound by the moments that slip away,
We walk the paths where memories sway.
In hidden layers, our souls connect,
An intricate dance, deep and perfect.

Through the fabric of dreams, we glide,
With unseen threads as our guide.
In every heartbeat, a pulse of gold,
In every story, the truth unfolds.

Invisible bond, yet crystal clear,
In the quiet places, I feel you near.
Through vast expanses, through time we blend,
On unseen threads, together we mend.

In the tapestry worn, our fibers glow,
Through darkest nights, a gentle flow.
In every heartbeat, in every sigh,
On unseen threads, we learn to fly.

Seasons of Affinity

In spring the flowers bloom,
Awakening whispers low,
Joy dances in the air,
In colors vibrantly aglow.

Summer brings the sun's embrace,
Warmth settles in the skies,
Laughter rings in every place,
As time like a river flies.

Autumn leaves fall in grace,
Painting paths of gold and red,
Memories held in every space,
In sighs and tales we've said.

Winter wraps the world in peace,
A blanket soft and white,
In stillness, hearts find release,
Beneath the starry night.

Through seasons we find our way,
Together, hand in hand,
In every dawn, in every day,
A bond that will ever stand.

Heartstrings Entwined

In silent glances shared between,
Two souls that softly meet,
A melody that's sweet and keen,
In every heartbeat's beat.

Through trials faced, we never part,
With threads of warmth and light,
A tapestry woven from the heart,
In shadows and in bright.

The laughter spills in flowing streams,
A river that knows no end,
In whispered hopes and dreams,
We find a love that bends.

As seasons change and years unfold,
We'll dance through every storm,
With stories shared, forever told,
In love's gentle, true form.

Through every note, our song will play,
With echoes pure and clear,
In heartstrings twined, we'll find our way,
Together, year by year.

The Resonance of Us

In echoes soft, your laughter sings,
A harmony divine,
In every word, a warmth it brings,
As if our hearts align.

Through every doubt, through every fear,
We find our way anew,
In closeness felt, so crystal clear,
As love's embrace comes through.

The silence shared, a canvas vast,
Where colors blend as one,
In moments cherished, memories cast,
A journey just begun.

With every step, the world ignites,
In vibrant hues of trust,
Together soaring to new heights,
In the melody of us.

Our hearts in sync, a rhythm true,
In every pulse and sigh,
In the resonance that is me and you,
A love that will never die.

Radiant Connections

With every sunrise paints the dawn,
A masterpiece of gold,
In every glance, new worlds are born,
In stories yet untold.

Through storms we find a deeper shade,
In challenges we grow,
Like flowers thriving in the glade,
With strength and grace, we flow.

The laughter shared, a vivid hue,
A brushstroke on the air,
In every moment, bright and true,
A spark of joy laid bare.

Connections weave a cosmic thread,
Binding hearts in one,
In every tear and word that's said,
A journey just begun.

Together we shine, a radiant light,
In unity, we dance,
With every heartbeat, love takes flight,
In life's bright, wondrous glance.

A Quilt of Lost Echoes

In the twilight's gentle glow,
Memories stitched in time's soft thread.
Each patch a tale of long ago,
Whispers of words once gently said.

Faded voices dance in the night,
A melody of joy and pain.
Each sentiment lost from our sight,
Yet lives in the heart's refrain.

Beneath the stars, we weave our dreams,
A tapestry of love and loss.
In every corner, silence gleams,
A testament to what it costs.

The warmth of hands that held us close,
Now threads of memory tightly wound.
In each stitch, a heartfelt dose,
Of echoes that linger all around.

As we lay this quilt tonight,
Let every shadow find its place.
In the stillness, find the light,
A patchwork of our shared grace.

The Ethereal Ties

Across the vast, unending sky,
A thread of silver gleams so bright.
In laughter's call, we learn to fly,
Bound by the warmth of love's light.

Every heartbeat sings your name,
A symphony of souls entwined.
In joy and sorrow, one remains,
In every moment, love defined.

The river flows, our spirits dance,
In shadows deep and sunlight's gleam.
With every glance, we take the chance,
To build anew from every dream.

In whispered winds, our promises,
Float gently on the breath of night.
Each secret woven in this bliss,
Echoes of trust, a pure delight.

Together still, though miles may part,
In every beat, we find our way.
The ties that bind the beating heart,
Are ethereal, yet here to stay.

Fading Echoes of Togetherness

In the stillness of the dawn,
Whispers fade like morning mist.
Memories linger, then are gone,
In time's relentless, fleeting twist.

A laugh once shared, now distant call,
The warmth of togetherness lost.
In the silence, we feel it all,
Reflecting on the loving cost.

The photo frame collects the dust,
Where voices once filled every space.
Now just shadows, and dreams rust,
Fading echoes of a warm embrace.

Yet in the heart, there lies a spark,
A flame that never truly dies.
Through every trial, every dark,
The depth of love forever cries.

So as the echoes start to fade,
Hold close the threads of yesterday.
In every memory gently laid,
Together, still, we find our way.

Currents of Compassion

In the depths of silence shared,
Where kindness flows like gentle streams.
A heartbeat soft, always prepared,
To lift the soul with hopeful dreams.

Through every storm that life may toss,
A hand reaches out, warm and near.
In aching hearts, we bear the loss,
From currents deep, compassion's cheer.

With every tear, a bond is made,
In woven tales of love and strife.
Through every trial, hope won't fade,
A tapestry of shared life.

Together we rise, hand in hand,
In love's embrace, we find our way.
A gentle touch makes stillness grand,
In currents soft, we choose to stay.

So let compassion be our guide,
In every choice, in every part.
With hearts aligned and arms spread wide,
We weave the world, a loving art.

Mysteries of the Heart

In shadows deep, love finds its way,
A whisper soft, in night and day.
Unraveled threads, a tangled dance,
Each heartbeat sings, a fleeting chance.

Secrets shared beneath the stars,
Silence speaks, no need for scars.
The soul connects, through gaze and sigh,
Beyond the words, where dreams can fly.

Time stands still in moments rare,
Two souls entwined, a perfect pair.
With every glance, the world will fade,
In lover's arms, no need for trade.

Yet mystery lingers, soft and bright,
In every shadow, in every light.
Why do we crave what we cannot see?
The heart's own riddles, wild and free.

Through endless quests, we'll seek and roam,
In unknown paths, we'll find our home.
For love's a puzzle, curious art,
Forever woven, the mysteries of the heart.

Poetic Interludes

A fleeting thought, like wind it sways,
Words like petals, in soft sun's rays.
Each stanza breathes, with rhythm's flow,
Painted emotions, a vibrant glow.

In whispers soft, the verses play,
Chasing echoes, through night and day.
With ink-stained hands, we carve our dreams,
In written lines, the heart redeems.

Time's gentle hand, a tender guide,
Life's many hues, we cannot hide.
With every pause, a moment seized,
In poetic breaths, our souls are pleased.

Pages turn, a laughter shared,
In pauses filled, our hearts laid bare.
Words as bridges, connecting thought,
In every line, together caught.

With every verse, a story spun,
In shadows danced, in light we run.
The rhythmic pulse, a tune we sing,
In poetic interludes, the heart takes wing.

Stranger's Kindness

In crowded streets, a glance exchanged,
A smile ignites, our hearts unchained.
An open door, a hand to lend,
In fleeting moments, we find a friend.

The warmth of eyes, a silent vow,
To share the weight of here and now.
With simple gestures, bonds we weave,
In stranger's kindness, we believe.

A helping hand on troubled days,
In kindness found, we find our ways.
Each act a spark, a light to share,
In tender grace, we show we care.

Threads of fate, in colors bright,
Bring strangers close, in radiant light.
Through laughter shared or tears dried up,
A stranger's kindness fills our cup.

Let us remember, through all we do,
The strength in kindness, so pure and true.
For in this world, love's gentle art,
Lives on in every stranger's heart.

Metaphysical Encounters

In realms beyond, where shadows play,
Time unravels, guiding the way.
Through cosmic threads, we rise and fall,
In metaphysical dance, we hear the call.

The universe whispers in quiet tones,
Echoes of dreams, in celestial zones.
Planets align, in perfect grace,
In moments, we find our destined place.

With each heartbeat, the infinite sings,
Entwined in fate, the soul takes wings.
Stars that twinkle, stories unfold,
In every glance, a truth retold.

Dimensions cross in a silent sigh,
As spirits meet, in the vast, we fly.
A glance from afar, our paths collide,
In metaphysical wonders, we learn to glide.

So seek the whispers, the signs in the night,
For in every spark, there's hidden light.
In interconnectedness, our spirits rise,
Through metaphysical encounters, we touch the skies.

Reflections in the Soul's Mirror

In the stillness, shadows dance,
Whispers of dreams hold their chance.
Each glance reveals what lies beneath,
A tapestry of truths, we bequeath.

Moments linger, softly glow,
In silent depths, our fears will flow.
With courage drawn from deep inside,
We face the tides, no need to hide.

Fragments of time, they intertwine,
In mirrors bright, our souls align.
Echoes of laughter, tears that blend,
In sacred space, we find a friend.

Here in this realm of quiet grace,
We learn to trust, to embrace space.
Through every rise and every fall,
We discover truth, the greatest call.

In reflections clear, the heart's delight,
Illuminates the darkest night.
With every glance, we come to see,
The boundless love that sets us free.

A Symphony of Silent Understanding

In the hush, our spirits play,
Melodies formed in the light of day.
With knowing glances, hands entwined,
A quiet bond, uniquely designed.

Notes unspoken, yet deeply felt,
In every meeting, our hearts have dealt.
Through laughter's echo and gentle sighs,
We weave our truths, no need for lies.

Fingers trace paths of uncharted thoughts,
In this harmony, no lesson taught.
Each heartbeat whispers, loud and clear,
Understanding deepens when you draw near.

Simplicity forms the truest sound,
In silence, the depth of love is found.
Together we listen, together we learn,
In this symphony, our spirits yearn.

Bound by the threads of empathy's grace,
Together we wander, time cannot erase.
In a world of noise, our peace is sought,
In this silent bond, our souls are caught.

Starlit Conversations

Beneath the vast, celestial sea,
We share our dreams, just you and me.
With stars as witnesses, we unfold,
Secrets of hearts, both warm and bold.

Each twinkling light, a tale to tell,
In the night sky, where wishes dwell.
Conversations dance on cosmic waves,
Filling the air, the universe saves.

The moonlight whispers, soft and bright,
Illuminating paths with gentle light.
In every pause, connection grows,
Like petals opening, our laughter flows.

We read the constellations' lore,
In starlit moments, we seek for more.
With every glance, our spirits soar,
Adrift together, forever explored.

From dusk till dawn, our voices blend,
In these moments, there's no end.
Hand in hand, we greet the morn,
Through starlit skies, our love is born.

The Chorus of Our Echoes

In quiet chambers, echoes fall,
Whispers of moments, a distant call.
Each sound reflects our shared refrain,
A melody borne of joy and pain.

We sing with voices, both faint and strong,
Harmonies woven where we belong.
With every note, a memory stirs,
The chorus grows, as time occurs.

Through valleys deep and mountains high,
Our echoes dance beneath the sky.
In laughter's ring and sorrow's sighs,
Together we rise, together we fly.

In silver threads of twilight's hue,
Our lives intertwine, as heartbeats do.
Each echo carries what we've become,
In this chorus, we are never undone.

As dusk embraces, our song will swell,
In rhythmic heartbeat, all we can tell.
Through every shadow, light will remain,
The chorus lingers, our souls' refrain.

Ties that Bind

In shadows cast by glowing light,
We find the threads that hold us tight.
Through laughter shared and whispered dreams,
We weave a bond that softly gleams.

In moments fierce, when storms arise,
Our hearts unite, we brave the skies.
With every tear and joy combined,
We learn the strength of ties that bind.

Through trials faced and fears expressed,
In arms of love, we find our rest.
Together, souls can truly soar,
An endless dance on life's grand floor.

In silence shared, in glances bright,
We navigate the dark of night.
With every heartbeat, every sigh,
Our spirits soar, our hopes fly high.

Though time may shift, and paths may part,
The bonds we share reside in heart.
For in this life, come what may,
It's love that guides us day by day.

Serendipitous Encounters

A chance glance crossed a crowded street,
Fates entwined, our hearts did meet.
In fleeting moments, stories blend,
Strangers once, now trusted friends.

An open door, a smile exchanged,
In lives unknown, joy's found, unchained.
Each serendipity lovingly spun,
In life's vast web, we dance as one.

With whispers soft, we share our woes,
In laughter's arms, our spirit glows.
Each memory crafted, sweet and rare,
A thread of joy, a bond to share.

The universe conspires to align,
Two souls together, by design.
In moments fleeting, magic's found,
In heartbeats shared, love does abound.

So let us cherish every chance,
In serendipity, we find our dance.
Embrace the wondrous gifts it brings,
In every note, our hearts will sing.

Mosaic of Kinship

In vibrant hues, our stories blend,
A tapestry where paths extend.
With threads of laughter, threads of tears,
We craft a bond that lasts for years.

Each life a tile in life's grand art,
We fit together, never apart.
In colors bold and shades anew,
Mosaic kinship forms for you.

From whispers shared to dreams pursued,
The ties we shape, love's interlude.
With every moment, every glance,
We celebrate this life, this chance.

In family gatherings, warmth is found,
A dance of hearts, a joyous sound.
As seasons change, we grow and bend,
A living mosaic without end.

So let us honor what we create,
In every cherished moment fate.
The beauty found in kinship's light,
A symphony of hearts in flight.

Resonance of Lives

In echoes soft, our stories play,
Each heartbeat shares a vivid sway.
With whispers nestled in the air,
Resonance brews, a bond so rare.

As waves upon a tranquil shore,
Lives intertwine, forevermore.
Each laughter's note, a tender chime,
In harmony, we dance through time.

In trials faced and triumphs won,
We find our strength when we are one.
With every challenge, every test,
Together, we are truly blessed.

With every story deeply sown,
Resonance lingers, love has grown.
In shared embrace, we find our voice,
In unity, the heart's true choice.

So let this life be symphony,
A tapestry of you and me.
In resonance, a light so bright,
Our lives entwined, our spirits' flight.

The Language of Kindness

A smile shared when darkness falls,
Words that lift and gently call.
Small gestures spark a brighter day,
In silence, kindness finds its way.

Open hearts with gentle grace,
In every word, a warm embrace.
To listen close is truly rare,
A gift exchanged, a lasting care.

Kindness flows like rivers deep,
In tender moments, secrets keep.
With every act, the world renews,
And love's soft language, we choose.

A touch, a look, a heartfelt deed,
In simple forms, we plant the seed.
Through kindness, bridges we construct,
Together, hearts will always flourish.

So let's speak in kindness pure,
For in this language, we find sure.
A world transformed with every chance,
In kindness, we shall always dance.

Fusion of Two Paths

Two travelers roam with dreams in hand,
Each step taken on golden sand.
Their stories weave, a tapestry bright,
Together they forge a new light.

Winding roads that twist and turn,
In whispered hopes, their spirits burn.
Two hearts beating, echoes align,
In the journey, their souls entwine.

The beauty of paths, once unknown,
Now merged to create a home.
They dance through life, a graceful blend,
In every challenge, a hand to lend.

As seasons change and rivers flow,
In shared moments, love will grow.
Two paths unite, no longer apart,
In every heartbeat, a single heart.

An adventure crafted, true and rare,
Every laughter shared, a bond to bear.
In the fusion of paths, they find their way,
Together forever, come what may.

Synchronicity's Embrace

In fleeting moments, fate aligns,
A glance exchanged, two lives entwined.
When stars collide in cosmic dance,
A magic spun in chance romance.

Echoes whisper through tangled threads,
Each heartbeat leads where love now spreads.
Unseen forces pull them near,
In synchronicity, no room for fear.

The universe speaks in signs so clear,
Every path chosen brings them here.
Like puzzle pieces, perfectly fit,
In this embrace, the world feels lit.

Connections bloom like flowers rare,
In synchrony, a soul laid bare.
Moments crafted in delicate grace,
In twilight's arms, they find their place.

Through time and space, their journey flows,
In synchronicity, love only knows.
Together they dance, hearts open wide,
In this embrace, forever abide.

The Magic of Unspoken Bonds

In glances shared across the room,
A silent language starts to bloom.
Every heartbeat whispers loud,
A connection strong, no need for crowd.

Invisible threads pull hearts so close,
In quiet moments, love can expose.
They need no words, the truth is clear,
An unspoken bond that draws them near.

In the hush of night, a feeling grows,
In each heartbeat, the magic flows.
Through laughter bright and shadows cast,
Together they happen, moments amassed.

The comfort found in closeness shared,
A tapestry woven, love declared.
With every glance, a story told,
In silent vows, together they hold.

Unspoken bonds, a treasure rare,
In every sigh, they breathe the air.
Forever tied by threads unseen,
In this magic, their love evergreen.

Serenade of Shared Dreams

Whispers float on silver streams,
Underneath the starry beams.
Voices blend in gentle sighs,
Painting hopes in midnight skies.

Every glance, a secret shared,
Every heartbeat, love declared.
In the stillness, dreams take flight,
Guided gently by the night.

Hands entwined, we find our way,
Navigating through the gray.
With each step, a tale we weave,
In this moment, we believe.

Echoes of our laughter ring,
In the joy that silence brings.
As our souls begin to dance,
In the warmth of sweet romance.

Together we embrace the dawn,
Chasing shadows until they're gone.
In this serenade of grace,
We find magic in this place.

Embrace of Familiar Strangers

In the crowd, we share a glance,
A fleeting spark, a stolen chance.
Familiar eyes, yet worlds apart,
A silent dance within the heart.

Paths may cross, but time stands still,
Every moment, we feel the thrill.
Stories linger on the breeze,
In the spaces, memories freeze.

With whispered words, we bridge the gap,
Lost in thoughts, a gentle trap.
In the silence, comfort grows,
A bond that only the heart knows.

Every smile, a quiet plea,
To hold the moment, just to be.
In the folds of time, we'll find
The threads that weave our hearts aligned.

Though strangers on this winding road,
We share the weight of love's great load.
In the embrace, we drift and sway,
Unraveling the end of day.

A Dance of Celestial Hearts

Underneath the cosmic glow,
We intertwine, let feelings flow.
Stars above us start to gleam,
As we move like in a dream.

With each twirl, a spark ignites,
Bringing warmth to endless nights.
Gravity can't hold us down,
In this unity, we drown.

Dreams align in swirls of light,
Drawing us into the night.
With every breath, we feel the pull,
Our spirits dancing, beautiful.

Whispers travel on the air,
A melody beyond compare.
In this rhythm, time stands still,
Hearts united, we fulfill.

As the stars begin to fade,
In our hearts, the love we've made.
A dance that lingers evermore,
In celestial embrace, we soar.

Shadows in the Light

In the glow of fading day,
Shadows stretch and drift away.
Secrets linger in the dusk,
In the silence, an unspoken trust.

Footsteps echo on the ground,
In this stillness, peace is found.
Chasing dreams beneath the sun,
Confessions made, our hearts are one.

Every ray, a story told,
Of the brave and of the bold.
In the brightness, shadows play,
Reminding us of yesterday.

As we wander through the night,
Hand in hand, hearts burning bright.
In the comfort of shadows cast,
We find a home that's meant to last.

Together we will face the dawn,
Knowing love will carry on.
In the dance of dark and light,
We embrace our endless flight.

The Radiance of Kindred Hearts

In twilight glow, our laughter sings,
Connected souls, on gentle wings.
A bond so pure, it lights the night,
Together we chase the dawn's first light.

With every word, our spirits dance,
In silent pauses, there's a chance.
To weave our dreams, to share the sky,
In kindred hearts, we learn to fly.

Through stormy days, through gentle rain,
We find the beauty in the pain.
A strength that grows with every tear,
Through darkest hours, we draw near.

With hands entwined, we walk the shore,
Each step a whisper, forevermore.
The ocean's call, a timeless song,
Together we write where we belong.

In every glance, a world unfolds,
In stories shared, our truth retold.
With every heartbeat, love imparts,
The radiant warmth of kindred hearts.

Flowing Rivers of Emotion

In quiet streams, our feelings flow,
Through winding paths, the waters glow.
With every ripple, tales are spun,
In flowing rivers, two become one.

The currents twist, they ebb and sway,
In softest whispers, night and day.
Emotions stir, like leaves in flight,
In depths unseen, we find our light.

Beneath the surface, secrets lie,
In gentle waves, we learn to fly.
The heart's language, pure and true,
In flowing rivers, love breaks through.

The banks may shift, the tides may turn,
In every lesson, we shall learn.
With each embrace, the world unfurls,
In every tear, a jewel swirls.

So let us sail on waters deep,
In flowing rivers, our spirits keep.
Through laughter's echo, through sorrow's song,
In tides of emotion, we belong.

Pathways of the Heart

On winding trails, our footsteps trace,
In every moment, we find our place.
With whispered dreams beneath the trees,
Pathways of the heart bring us to peace.

With every turn, new wonders bloom,
In shadows cast, dispelling gloom.
The moonlight guides our wayward feet,
On pathways paved, our souls align, sweet.

In silence shared, our spirits soar,
Together exploring what lies in store.
Through thorns and blooms, we journey far,
With love as our compass, our guiding star.

With every heartbeat, bonds are sealed,
In golden moments, truth revealed.
Through paths unknown, we face the night,
In journey's grace, we find our light.

So here we stand, on sacred ground,
In every heartbeat, love is found.
In pathways of the heart, we tread,
A tapestry of lives, lovingly spread.

Luminescence in Union

In gentle whispers, shadows blend,
A dance of light, where hearts extend.
With souls ignited in vibrant hue,
Luminescence in union, we renew.

The stars above, they brightly gleam,
In every glance, a shared dream.
With hands that touch, and spirits free,
In radiant glow, we cease to be.

Through storms of doubt, our anchor's firm,
In love's embrace, we find our term.
Each beam of light, a promise shines,
In unity's warmth, the heart aligns.

With every laugh, with every sigh,
Our love transcends, it soars on high.
In every moment, the magic's found,
In luminescence, our hearts unbound.

As day meets night, we find our way,
With every beat, come what may.
In union's glow, we softly soar,
In luminescence, forevermore.

Embrace of Kindred

In twilight's glow, we find our way,
Hearts entwined, as night meets day.
A whispered bond, a sacred trust,
In every glance, love's gentle gust.

With open arms, we share our fears,
Laughter dances, drying tears.
Together we weave a tapestry bright,
Warmed by the soft, nurturing light.

In solitude, we stand as one,
Under the canvas of the sun.
Every moment, a treasure to hold,
In kindred spirit, stories told.

Through storms we pass, side by side,
In unity, our hearts abide.
With every step, we pave the way,
For love's embrace, come what may.

So here we stand, hand in hand,
In this beautiful, timeless land.
Together we rise, together we thrive,
In the embrace of kindred, we come alive.

Echoes in the Void

In silence deep, we hear the call,
Whispers linger in the hall.
Shadows flicker, light retreats,
In the void, where silence meets.

Lost in thoughts that drift like mist,
Moments fade, they can't be kissed.
Yet the echoes find their way,
Through the darkness, they convey.

Within the void, a spark ignites,
Dreams take flight on starry nights.
In solitude, we find our grace,
A journey deep, an endless space.

With every heartbeat, whispers grow,
Guiding us through all we know.
Echoes dance, a haunting tune,
In the void, beneath the moon.

So catch the echoes, let them soar,
Through the stillness, we explore.
In every silence, we create,
A world alive, a whispered fate.

Dance of the Intimate

In the quiet, shadows blend,
Two souls align, hearts transcend.
A tender touch, a shared sigh,
In this dance, we learn to fly.

Softly we move, a gentle sway,
In rhythm's pulse, we drift away.
Eyes locked tight, a woven spell,
In every heartbeat, stories dwell.

No words needed, our spirits sing,
In the melody, a sacred ring.
With every twirl, we lose our fear,
In the dance, only love draws near.

Through the night, we spin and glide,
In laughter's joy, we take the ride.
Each step a promise, each turn a chance,
In the embrace of this intimate dance.

So let us sway till the morning light,
With every breath, we hold on tight.
In this dance, we find our trance,
In love's rhythm, we forever prance.

Bridging Heartbeats

Two worlds collide and intertwine,
Each heartbeat echoes, yours and mine.
Across the chasm, we reach out,
In this bond, we cast all doubt.

With every pulse, a promise made,
In the stillness, fears will fade.
Steps aligned, we journey far,
Together we weave, a shooting star.

In whispered dreams, we find our way,
A bridge of love, come what may.
Through valleys low, and mountains high,
Hand in hand, we dare to fly.

Every heartbeat a step we take,
In the silence, we bend and break.
Yet through the night, we forge ahead,
In this dance, no words are said.

So let us build on this foundation,
With every beat, a celebration.
Together we stand, never apart,
Bridging heartbeats, two into one heart.

Unraveling the Distance

Through shadows long and whispers faint,
Hearts beat across the wide expanse.
With every star, a promise shared,
In silent hopes, our spirits dance.

Miles fade away with dreams in flight,
Each breath of wind, a soft embrace.
In tangled paths, our souls align,
And love's resolve shall find its place.

The night grows deep with yearning light,
As constellations draw us near.
In woven threads of time and space,
We unravel distance, soft and clear.

A bridge of thoughts, forever strong,
In every moment, we reside.
Between the worlds, we find our song,
Together, no more need to hide.

So let the stars be our guide now,
With open hearts, we chase the glow.
For in the dark, our love will shine,
Unraveling distance, two in flow.

Intergalactic Friendship

In the vastness of the night sky,
Feelings soar on cosmic winds.
Stars twinkle bright like laughter shared,
In this realm, where friendship begins.

Across the galaxies we roam,
Finding wonders, hand in hand.
In orbits wide, we laugh and dream,
Intergalactic, love so grand.

The moonlight bathes our journey bright,
In stardust trails, our voices blend.
With every pulse that lights the dark,
A bond that time will never end.

From quasar tales to comet's path,
Our adventures touch the heart.
In every dance of the universe,
Friendship's light will never part.

So let's explore this endless space,
With joy and laughter as our guide.
In every star, a memory made,
Intergalactic, side by side.

Under the Celestial Canvas

Beneath the stars, a canvas sprawls,
Brushstrokes of dreams, a cosmic art.
With every glimmer, stories told,
In silence, painting heart to heart.

The Milky Way, a river wide,
Where spirit flows and beauty shows.
Each twinkling star inside our minds,
Guides our journey as it goes.

In twilight's glow, the colors blend,
Soft whispers of the night unfold.
With every glance, creation stirs,
New tales of love and hope retold.

We lay beneath this boundless sky,
With dreams that echo through the night.
Finding peace in the vast unknown,
Our hearts aligned, our spirits light.

So paint your wishes on the stars,
Let them soar on gentle winds.
Together, under this celestial dome,
We'll find a world that never ends.

Synchronicity at Twilight

As daylight fades to dusky hue,
All things align, the world feels right.
In whispers soft, we find our way,
Synchronicity graces the night.

Time dances slow, in moments shared,
With stars emerging, soft and bright.
Each glance a spark, a secret coded,
The universe whispers, "Hold on tight."

In twilight's glow, our paths converge,
Hidden threads weave through the air.
With every heartbeat in this space,
We know, together, we're almost there.

So now let's breathe in the dusk's embrace,
With fate entwined, we rise, we flow.
In synchronicity, we take our flight,
Through twilight's veil, our spirits glow.

In every shadow, light reveals,
The dance of life, a wondrous art.
When night and day share a secret smile,
We'll find the magic in our heart.

Fireside Dialogues

In the glow of embers bright,
Whispers dance in smoky night.
Stories weave through time and space,
Heartfelt truths we all embrace.

Echoes of laughter fill the air,
Memories linger, joys we share.
Voices soft, yet strong and clear,
In this warmth, we have no fear.

Each flicker sparks a tale untold,
Wisdom shared, both young and old.
With every crackle, dreams take flight,
Binding souls in gentle light.

Glimmers of hope in twilight's shroud,
Lives connect, both meek and proud.
A tapestry of hearts aligned,
At this fireside, love we find.

As shadows stretch and night unfolds,
The stories linger, warmth it holds.
In the silent night, we breathe,
Fireside whispers, hearts reprieve.

Language of the Heart

Soft murmurs speak without a sound,
In silence, love is truly found.
A gentle glance, a tender sigh,
In every touch, the heart's reply.

Words unspoken weave their thread,
Connecting souls, where dreams are fed.
Emotions dance in vibrant hues,
A canvas painted with our truths.

In every heartbeat, stories lie,
Beyond the stars, our spirits fly.
A symphony of warmth and grace,
In every breath, you find your place.

The language formed from every tear,
In joy and pain, we draw you near.
With whispered hopes and soft refrains,
The heart's sweet song, forever reigns.

Through every heartbeat, love will flow,
In every glance, together grow.
Our language speaks, so pure, so free,
In the depths of you and me.

Crossroads of Being

At twilight's edge, we stand alone,
Decisions weighed, like scattered stones.
Paths diverge in soft, dim light,
What lies ahead? We hold on tight.

With every step, the future calls,
Echoes linger within these walls.
Choices made and bridges burned,
In this moment, lessons learned.

The crossroads hum with dreams and fear,
Unraveled hopes whispering near.
Each road a tale yet to be spun,
A journey shared, or one undone.

Winds of change curl round our feet,
Guiding hearts, we feel the beat.
In uncertainty, we find our core,
Embrace the unknown, forever explore.

In every choice, a chance to grow,
In every doubt, the spark to glow.
At this crossroads, we become,
The stories written, yet to come.

Essence Exchange

In the depth of quiet gaze,
Lies a world where hearts ablaze.
Connection forged in subtle grace,
An essence shared in silent space.

In fleeting moments, truths arise,
Unspoken vows beneath the skies.
With every breath, we trade our fears,
The bond we weave through all the years.

Like rivers flowing, souls entwine,
A sacred dance, both yours and mine.
In laughter's echo, we unite,
A symphony of pure delight.

With whispered kindness, love expands,
An essence exchanged in gentle hands.
In this communion, hearts take flight,
Together shining in the light.

The essence of all that we are,
A guiding light, a fleeting star.
In every heartbeat, we exchange,
A love that time cannot estrange.

In the Company of Stars

Under the blanket of night, we gaze,
Whispers of dreams in silver rays.
Constellations dance in the deep,
Secrets of time in silence keep.

With every twinkle, tales unfold,
Ancient stories, in whispers told.
Guiding our hearts through paths unknown,
In the vastness, we find our home.

In solitude's warmth, we share our fears,
Each shining light, a comfort near.
Together we walk on celestial tide,
In the company of stars, we abide.

At dawn's arrival, their glow shall fade,
Yet their warmth within us stays unmade.
For every moment that we lost,
In the night's embrace, we learned the cost.

So we cherish this cosmic flow,
A bond that only the night can know.
Hand in hand, as worlds collide,
In the company of stars, we confide.

Tapestry of Souls

In the weave of time, we are threads,
Connected by choices, the paths we've tread.
Each soul a color, vibrant and bright,
Creating a tapestry in the night.

Somewhere in silence, our stories blend,
Moments of joy, on which we depend.
Stitches of laughter, tears softly trace,
In this grand fabric, we find our place.

With every heartbeat, we spin anew,
Diverse and unique, in all that we do.
In shadows and light, we learn to be whole,
Threads of compassion, weaving a soul.

As seasons change, our patterns shift,
Yet love remains the timeless gift.
In the garden of life, we bloom and grow,
A tapestry of souls, sewn in love's glow.

So let us embrace this intricate dance,
As we twine together in life's expanse.
In the fabric of hope, our spirits arise,
A masterpiece forged under endless skies.

Beneath the Same Sky

Under the arch of the vast, blue dome,
We search for warmth, a place called home.
With every heartbeat, our spirits unite,
Beneath the same sky, stars burning bright.

In distant lands, our paths may stray,
Yet whispers of love always find a way.
Though rivers may part us, we share the breeze,
In every sunset, we find our ease.

As night descends, we look above,
Beneath the same sky, we feel the love.
Constellations witness our dreams take flight,
Guided by passion and the moon's pure light.

In times of sorrow, when shadows loom,
We find solace in the stars' soft bloom.
For we are not alone in our plight,
Beneath the same sky, we share the night.

Together we rise, hands stretched wide,
In the universe's warmth, we now confide.
Though distance may linger like clouds on high,
We stand united beneath the same sky.

Confluence of Journeys

In the rivers of life, our paths entwine,
Flowing together, your journey and mine.
With every twist and turn we take,
A confluence born, decisions we make.

Through valleys of joy and mountains of pain,
We wander as one, through sunshine and rain.
In shared laughter and tears we find,
The strength of a bond, forever aligned.

As seasons change, and time ebbs away,
The stories we tell will never decay.
In the heart's embrace, we gather the light,
A confluence of journeys, shining bright.

On this winding road, we find our way,
With every sunrise igniting the day.
In the dance of fate, we twirl and sway,
Together we journey, come what may.

So let us cherish this sacred flow,
Where the rivers converge, our spirits grow.
In the tapestry of life, we stride,
A confluence of journeys, side by side.

Celestial Conversations

Whispers dance among the stars,
The moonlight wraps our dreams in gold.
Constellations spin their tales,
In silence, stories unfold.

Galaxies meet in gentle sighs,
A cosmic bond we cannot see.
Winds of fate weave timeless threads,
Connecting you and me.

Meteor trails paint the dark,
Guiding wishes through the night.
Each twinkle holds a fleeting spark,
A moment caught in light.

In twilight's glow, our hearts converse,
Each breath a note in this sweet song.
Endless sighs, the universe,
In dreams, we truly belong.

So let us wander through the skies,
With celestial thoughts in play.
For in this vast expanse we rise,
Together, come what may.

Union of Dreams

In sleep's embrace, our visions blend,
A tapestry of hopes entwined.
Night's canvas glows with hues of gold,
Where heart and mind are aligned.

We float on waves of starlit grace,
Unified in a world apart.
Each dream a thread in passion's lace,
Stitching realms within the heart.

Bound by whispers of the night,
Together we explore the vast.
In shadows deep, we find our light,
A union formed to ever last.

With every heartbeat, worlds are born,
Each sigh a step on cosmic ground.
In this realm, our spirits soar,
Where love's true essence can be found.

Awake or lost in reverie,
In dreams, we find our sacred place.
Forever joined, just you and me,
A union time cannot erase.

Intertwined Paths

Through tangled woods our journeys trace,
Two wandering souls led by the light.
With every turn, we share a fate,
In step with shadows, day and night.

The whispers of the leaves in air,
Guide us along this winding way.
Each footprint left, a silent prayer,
A promise made that we will stay.

Beneath the stars, our paths will cross,
Bound by the threads of dreams we weave.
In every gain, in every loss,
Together strong, we do believe.

Through storms that threaten, winds that wail,
Our hearts remain forever near.
With every step, we will not fail,
In unity, we conquer fear.

When daylight fades and shadows call,
Our intertwined paths shall not part.
In this vast world, together, we stand tall,
Two souls, one boundless heart.

Shared Breath of Life

In quiet moments, breath we share,
A soft exchange beneath the sky.
In every sigh, love's warmth laid bare,
Inhale the truth, let worries fly.

With every heartbeat, rhythms blend,
Unspoken vows beneath the stars.
A sacred bond that will not end,
With every breath, we heal our scars.

The pulse of nature runs through veins,
As time dissolves in gentle flow.
Together, dancing through our pains,
In unity, we learn to grow.

Upon this path our spirits meet,
In shared moments, joy ignites.
With open hearts, we find our beat,
Two lives entwined in endless nights.

So let us breathe, feel life's embrace,
In every kiss, a silent prayer.
In this journey, we find our place,
Together, in the love we share.

Landscapes of Longing

In valleys deep, where shadows play,
A whisper calls, then drifts away.
Beneath the stars, my heart does roam,
In quiet woods, I seek my home.

The mountains rise, they touch the sky,
With every breath, I ache to fly.
Through rivers wild, my thoughts will flow,
To distant shores, where dreams can grow.

The golden fields that stretch so wide,
In every grain, my hopes reside.
Each sunset paints a tale unwound,
A promise held in fertile ground.

Yet storms will come, and shadows loom,
For every heart must face its gloom.
But in the light, I often find,
A thread of hope that's intertwined.

So here I stand, in this embrace,
With nature's hand, I find my place.
In landscapes vast, my soul takes flight,
And longs for peace within the night.

Glimpses of the Divine

In morning light, the dew does gleam,
A fleeting touch, a whispered dream.
Through fragrant blooms, the spirit soars,
In sacred moments, love restores.

The hills alive with song and grace,
In nature's arms, I find my space.
With every wave that kisses sand,
I glimpse the touch of a greater hand.

The stars above, a timeless guide,
In every twinkle, hope abides.
A gentle breeze, a soft caress,
In these small gifts, I find my bless.

Through quiet nights and fragrant blooms,
The heart expands, dispels the glooms.
In every sigh, the spirit gleans,
A tapestry of sacred scenes.

The laughter shared, a sacred tie,
In every moment, we reach the sky.
With open hearts, we touch the divine,
In every soul, a light will shine.

Connections Beyond Time

In echoes soft, our voices blend,
With woven threads that transcend.
Across the years, a bond we share,
In every glance, a memory rare.

Through paths we've walked and trials faced,
In every hug, a warmth embraced.
A smile exchanged, a touch so light,
In every heartbeat, love takes flight.

As seasons change and rivers flow,
Our hearts entwined, forever grow.
In laughter shared and tears we shed,
Our spirits dance, where passions led.

With whispered dreams and hopes held dear,
In every moment, you are near.
The canvas bright, as time unwinds,
In shades of love, our soul reminds.

And though the world may drift away,
In silent moments, we will stay.
For time is but a fleeting friend,
In every breath, our love transcends.

Soft Echoes of Togetherness

In cozy rooms, where shadows blend,
We share our thoughts, around the bend.
With laughter light, and joy aglow,
In every corner, memories grow.

As twilight falls, the candles gleam,
In gentle whispers, we chase a dream.
A tapestry of moments spun,
Together we rise, two hearts as one.

The warmth of hands, a tender touch,
In silent gazes, we say so much.
Through storms that rage, and trials near,
In every heartbeat, we conquer fear.

With every story shared at night,
In simple joys, we find our light.
The world outside may spin away,
But in this space, we choose to stay.

So let the days chase after night,
In every glance, our love ignites.
With soft echoes of our embrace,
We find in time, our sacred space.

The Heart's Vibration

In shadows deep, the pulse does beat,
A silent song, where two hearts meet.
The whispers carried on the breeze,
A dance of souls that aims to please.

With every thrum, a dream ignites,
A tapestry of shared delights.
The rhythm swells, a tender trance,
In every glance, a sweet romance.

As echoes fade, the bonds grow tight,
Their essence woven, pure and bright.
Together wrapped in time's embrace,
A journey shared, a sacred space.

With every beat, the world aligns,
Their hearts entwined, like ancient signs.
Resonating through the night,
A melody of love's pure light.

In silence held, their spirits race,
Upon the winds, in endless grace.
Eternal flames, forever fanned,
Two vessels joined, a love so grand.

Ethereal Touchstones

Glimmers shine in twilight's glow,
Whispers dance where soft winds blow.
With every spark, a truth unfolds,
In secret places, fate beholds.

The stones we gather, precious gems,
Reflecting life like rare diadems.
Each moment held, a fragile pause,
Where time dissolves, without a cause.

In quiet realms, their voices call,
Threads of fate in a cosmic sprawl.
A gentle touch, the universe feels,
With every heart, a truth reveals.

Through hazy mists, the vision sways,
In wonderlost, the spirit plays.
An endless quest, the soul dives deep,
Into the dreams that time will keep.

These touchstones guide our weary way,
Through night's embrace and brightened day.
They hold our hopes, they weave our fears,
In every laugh, in all our tears.

Unfolding Connections.

Threads of silver, gently twine,
Each moment shared, a sacred sign.
In laughter soft, and quiet sighs,
The fabric grows as spirit flies.

Hand in hand, we journey slow,
Through valleys low and peaks aglow.
Connections bloom in vibrant hues,
In every path, a life anew.

Through every turn, the bonds will weave,
A tapestry of love to weave.
With every step, our hearts align,
In traces left, the world's design.

Roots entwined in earth's embrace,
Unfolding dreams in secret space.
With open hearts, we cultivate,
Each bond a seed, a destined fate.

In whispered thoughts, our spirits fly,
Connections strong beneath the sky.
Together we mend the world's seam,
In every heartbeat, love's pure dream.

Whispers of the Unseen

In twilight hush, the world can hear,
The subtle tones that draw us near.
With every sigh, a story spins,
In shadowed light, the magic begins.

Beneath the stars, a song unfolds,
With tales of hope that life beholds.
In gentle winds, they drift and sway,
Whispers soft, calling us to play.

The unseen paths we often tread,
Hold secrets of the words unsaid.
In silent moments, connections bloom,
Finding solace in the room.

As daylight fades, the muse appears,
In quiet hearts, the truth adheres.
No need for words, just knowing glances,
In unison, the spirit dances.

Through woven dreams, they come alive,
In hidden realms where thoughts derive.
With every glance, a legacy,
In whispers shared, our souls run free.

Intertwined Journeys

Two paths once parted, now align,
We walk together, fate divine.
With every step, our stories blend,
Creating memories that won't end.

Side by side, we face the road,
Each weight lifted, shared load.
In shadows cast, we find the light,
Together we embrace the night.

Through winding trails, our laughter flows,
In every heart, a garden grows.
Roots entangled beneath the ground,
In every moment, love is found.

As seasons change, we'll still be near,
A bond unbroken, crystal clear.
Through storms and sunshine, hand in hand,
A timeless dance upon the sand.

From mountains high to valleys low,
In every stride, our spirits grow.
With every dawn, a chance to soar,
Our intertwined journeys, forevermore.

Sunbeams on Shared Paths

Golden lights in morning's glow,
Shimmering dreams in daylight's flow.
Together we chase the fleeting rays,
In laughter and joy, our hearts ablaze.

Upon the trails of sunlit bliss,
We gather moments, a tender kiss.
Each cherished laugh, a twinkling spark,
Guiding us gently through the dark.

Whispers of warmth in every breeze,
Time stands still among the trees.
Hand in hand, we draw so near,
With every heartbeat, love appears.

In twilight's glow, we pause to rest,
Memories woven in every quest.
A tapestry of futures bright,
Guided by sunbeams and delight.

Forever etched in golden hues,
Our path together, love infused.
Through sunlight's dance, our spirits rise,
In shared paths, we touch the skies.

Silent Offerings

In quiet moments, we exchange,
The beauty found in hearts unchained.
A glance, a smile, a gentle nod,
In silence, we walk the path of God.

We gather whispers, soft as air,
In unspoken truths, we lay bare.
Every heartbeat, a gift we share,
In the stillness, love is rare.

Beneath the stars, our dreams entwine,
In hushed reverence, your hand in mine.
With every breath, a sacred vow,
In silence, we honor the now.

Through unseen threads, our souls connect,
In tender moments, we reflect.
Silent offerings, pure and true,
In each heartbeat, I find you.

Together we thrive in the gentle light,
In corners dim, our spirits bright.
In the quiet, we build our song,
In silent offerings, we belong.

Mosaic of Togetherness

Fragments of moments, colors collide,
In every shadow, we confide.
Each piece a story, a life we've shared,
In this mosaic, love is declared.

With every laugh, we paint a hue,
In brushstrokes bold, we see what's true.
Together we rise, despite the fall,
Each shard a testament, we stand tall.

Textures and shades woven with care,
In unity's dance, we're always there.
Through trials faced, our spirits blend,
In the art of togetherness, we mend.

Every heartbeat adds to the scene,
A tapestry woven, vibrant and keen.
In harmony's rhythm, we find our place,
In this mosaic, our love's embrace.

Together we thrive, a shared design,
In every fragment, your heart is mine.
As the picture forms, we find our way,
In this mosaic, come what may.

9 789916 891032